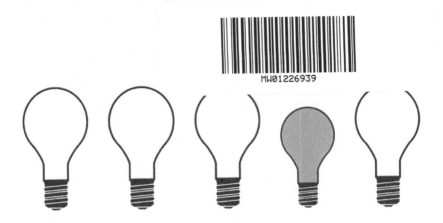

# WHAT LITTLE

# I KNOW NOW

## A view from the back nine of life

### Linda B. Myers

Tod –
Sometimes you
Just have to
laugh

Linda B Myers

Published by Mycomm One
© 2024 Linda B. Myers

ISBN: 978-1-7352477-2-4

Cover design by Alan Halfhill
Interior design by Heidi Hansen

For updates and chatter:
www.LindaBMyers.com
Facebook.com/lindabmyers.author
myerslindab@gmail.com

# Table of Contents

# DEDICATION

To the people and places I've admired along the way.

## SPECIAL THANKS

To Michael Dashiell
Editor, Sequim Gazette

# INTRODUCTION

*"Selfless and self-effacing, Linda Myers has an uncanny ability to both surprise her readers and draw us into the familiar. Her writing is a treasure."*
Michael Dashiell, Editor, Sequim Gazette.

The articles you have in your hands are taken from eight years of my newspaper opinion pieces in my local *Sequim Gazette.* The column is called *From the Back Nine*, but it is not about golf. For all of you wearing pants in bad plaids or mistaking this for the sports page, I apologize.

These articles are viewpoints and observations from someone on the back nine of life. They are not a memoir so much as a consideration of the distances we travel.

I have reached the age when I actually think about things like insurance with a prescription benefit. I never pass up a clean restroom. I consider shopping at Walmart to be an extreme sport. I don't much care anymore whether anyone thinks I'm too fat or too opinionated or too indecisive or too anything.

It is a very freeing time of life. Come along with me for a while.

# SECTION ONE

# Through the Ages

# GOLD IN THE GOLDEN YEARS

A young person asked me: "Are there any good sides to getting old? I would love to hear about one of those for a change." Fair enough, young person. Here goes:

- I am delighted not to be you. I've been through your youthful angst and don't want to survive it again. It's the pits. In general, old people are far more tranquil; we've found our answers, for better or worse. You will, too, in the fullness of time. It's very freeing.

- I no longer worry about getting pregnant (a short digression: I was young in the age of coat hanger abortions ... I grieve you may soon face that, too).

- I am not obliged to X, post, like, snap, or tumble. It is not a mandatory part of the silver-hair culture. It is merely assumed I don't know how to X, post, etc., at my age. Not nice, but not hurtful. But for you? If you don't snap, like, etc. it is assumed you are the biggest loser in the popularity department. I guess the moral of this is that life never gets fair, but it does get to the point where you don't give a fig.

- Nobody laughs if I don't follow a fashion trend, in fact they would laugh if I did. I like jeans that come up to my waist and don't have holes in the knees when I purchase them. If I have a bad hair day it is exactly like every other day. 'Fitting in' is not the driving force it used to be. You will love it, my young friend.

- Wardrobe needs are very narrow. No prom or wedding dresses for me. One dress or suit. Dressing is cheap and easy.

- When you are sick, you can stay home until you are well. You are not under the gun to get back to work.

- I have no career goals. If I am found stabbed in the back, you will know a coworker didn't do it. I don't have coworkers anymore.

- Anxiety and stress are miserable regardless of your age. But time pressure is less debilitating these days. I can take the dog for a walk later. Unpacking can wait another day. In the greater sense, time is shorter, of course. But tick to tock, not every second is jammed with must-get-dones.

- Like Blanche DuBois, I now depend on the kindness of others. Unlike Blanche, I often get it. Someone with a younger back carries the heavier suitcases.

- I get a bucket of pleasure out of very little. A parrot with a Popsicle stick ... a big batch of library books ... a groaner from my brother-in-law ... sitting and looking at all the marvels there are to sit and look at on the Olympic Peninsula. Gosh, with so much to do, I might start feeling pressured again. I better go take a nap.

# THE AGE OF CUTENESS

There are many signs of aging that we all know are going to happen, come what may. These signs involve strange spots that weren't there yesterday, wild hairs tough as boar bristles, a memory that floats just out of your reach, or enough excess skin to incubate a penguin egg.

But there is one sign of aging here on the back nine that has surprised me: I have an ever-increasing desire for cute clothing. You know, the kind you had as a little kid. Is this, in fact, a return to childhood? Emm, maybe. I'm more inclined to think that it is a return to a time so simple that a small touch of sweetness could actually make you happy. Life kind of takes that out of you.

I've spent my whole adult life in tailored business casual, avoiding ruffly blouses with embroidered daisies on the collars or humorous slogans emblazoned across my chest. Okay, maybe a school logo but never anything like *Dear Santa: Could you define good?* But just lately, I find a hankering for the sweatshirt (excuse me, I mean fleece) that maybe sports an embroidered polar bear in a scarf with real fringe. Or a row of flamingos prancing around the hem of my cruise wear. God help me, I actually *have* cruise wear.

My closet is now full of happy with beaded birdies and sequined gardens and appliquéd flip flops. I still stop short of puppies and bunnies, but I confess I have needlepoint ladybugs on my slippers. Again, I apologize.

Speaking of shoes, if there is any definitive proof of the old Mars/Venus theory, it is in the shoe department. No man understands what every woman knows about shoes. Trust me, the collector desire in this category gets worse as you get older. Shoes with stripes, wild colors, bows, charms, tassels. Stilettos, platforms, wedges, flats, boots. There is no limit to this lust until a medical professional one day says to you, "For heaven's sake, if you keep falling off them, quit wearing them."

The Age of Cuteness blindsided me. It was kind of a return to those thrilling days of yesteryear, when childhood was so damn much fun. What a joyful surprise to discover it waiting here for me on the back nine all along.

# MY MOTHER'S POCKETBOOK

When I was a child my mother carried a pocketbook everywhere, not unlike Queen Elizabeth. It was always hard-sided and short-handled, and it opened or closed with a definite SNAP from the bear-trap closure of its metal toggle. No kid could get into that purse unnoticed, not if your mother had the kind of hearing that could locate your dog tiptoeing into the neighbor's yard. "GET BACK HERE!" she'd yell from the back porch, and Kiltie or Folly or Zipper would slink home, awed by the Human with Ears of a Bat.

But this isn't about my mother's ears; it's about her pocketbook. It was as magical as Narnia, a land that could expand to fill any requirement a five-year-old might have.

Our car for road trips from Michigan to Montana was always a Buick with a backseat the size of a California King. Sis and I could lie on the floor reading comics or sit on the seat and play Sorry, the boardgame spread out between us. Anything like a kiddy car-seat had yet to be dreamed of. Inevitably we would get bored, and if we'd been good, up there in the front seat the magic pocketbook might open.

Blackjack or Clove Gum would appear, or Butter Rum Lifesavers. Adult-ish flavors that still had enough sugar to rocket us to the roof. Sometimes Mom had horehound which was a gut-wrenching disappointment, but if that happened there were usually restorative lemon drops, one for each of us. Maybe we'd get to play with her compact so we could powder our noses until we sneezed. Often, we shared the pair of clip-on earrings she'd tucked in her pocketbook after they hurt her lobes. The pocketbook was a complete general store, always with Kleenex, Band-Aids, folding plastic rain bonnets, toothpicks, and safety pins.

My mother has been gone for many years. Recently, Sis and I cleared out a whole pile of our own purses; apparently neither of us was ever capable of throwing one out when you could just as easily jam it back into a closet. At the bottom of the pile was an unassuming medium brown bag. You guessed it … one of Mom's. Her last one, in fact, an item we couldn't discard but could, after the passing of time, forget.

Sis opened it. All that was left inside was an ancient Avon Lip Balm and a spiral-bound Mead notebook, one about the dimensions of an index card. Inside Mom had copied down a verse that was written by Henry Van Dyke, 19th century American poet. Her tiny, neat longhand read:

> Time is too slow for those who wait,
> Too swift for those who fear,
> Too long for those who grieve,
> Too short for those who rejoice.
> But for those who love, time is Eternity.

I read those few simple lines. And just like that, I was transformed again to the days in the back seat when the best of magic would come to me from my mother's pocketbook.

# EXPOSURE TO THE ARTS

The Mister and I lived in Chicago for many years. Now and then my niece would come from Oregon for a visit. I was always eager to find something really cool to do, especially once she reached the sophistication of the middle school years.

I knew she loved scary books and movies, the bloodier the better. This desire to scare yourself stupid is apparently a trait passed from aunt to niece vs mother to daughter. Her mother wouldn't take her to scary flicks having never recovered from them in her own youth, but I always loved them. As a child at the Saturday matinees, I enjoyed a brain attached to one floating eyeball kept alive in a tank of goo. Or the tingler sucking precious bodily fluids from your spine. While the rest of my family judged movies on a five star system, I judged them on a five nightmare system. Bottom line, scary stuff was a safe bet for my niece and me to share. And definitely cool.

Back to Chicago. I looked through the *Tribune* to find something she, her Uncle Roger, and I could all do together. And there it was: a tiny ad for a Clive Barker play, appearing in one of Chicago's numerous neighborhood theatres. I don't remember the name of the play but this was Clive Barker. Guaranteed to be full of ghoulies and ghosties and long legged beasties.

The theatre was tiny, in a basement with folding chairs if memory serves. Because nobody else was there who wasn't family of the cast, we three were treated like royalty. We were moved down to the first row. We could rest our elbows on the stage.

It turned out the play did not have aliens ripping out of chest walls or zombies returning from the grave. It involved many men in prison dressed in priest-like robes, with one dude in serious need of anti-psychotic meds. A play about men in prison is likely to have themes you'd rather not share with your niece. I began to worry.

Suddenly, one cast member threw off his robe and was totally nude. I repeat: totally nude. And he played to his audience. The footlights must have given him fairly serious burns. Let me just say his privates were no longer private.

I looked at Roger. He was looking down to contemplate his cuticles and didn't look up again for several days. I babbled at length about the weather on the drive home.

I'm pretty sure that my niece has a memory or two she hopes I never shared with her Mom. But that evening, I created a memory I hope SHE never shared with her Mom. It's about the night I exposed her daughter to the arts.

# MELLOW MOTHERING

I own my mother's five-year diaries. She kept them from 1952 until she died in 1999. You know the kind of thing – not a journal with blank pages but four lines for each year and five years of the same date all on one page. A tiny bit of space for a whole day.

Since those diaries are about my life as well as hers, I wanted to own them. You never outgrow your need for your mother's comfort, and I thought of the years ahead. I would pull them out and enjoy them and remember her with love. She would have preferred to be buried with them, but I did some very unflattering begging. They were her final gift to me.

I must admit my mother's diaries present me as a woebegone sort of child, and I am not sure she always showed the proper amount of parental concern for my sensitive little self. For instance:

*April 17, 1955: Lovely day. Bill helped Johnnie start breezeway. Then we went to Irene's for dinner. Girls rode horses – Linda fell off.* Wouldn't you think she might have mentioned whether I was OK? I know there are only four lines per day, but was I crushed under the hooves of a thundering stallion? She could have at least replaced that breezeway stuff with something like "O! My poor darling girl." A casual approach to my traumas seems to be a thread through the early years. For instance, this from a vacation in Florida:

*February 21, 1954: Lots of rain today. Linda got stung by a Man-o-war. Badly. We had red snapper dinner for 14 on our patio. Betty & Mike visited until late this eve.* I remember the Man o' War incident as far more gut wrenching than Ma gave it credit. I was surrounded by searing tentacles, then got my hands severely stung trying to pick them off. A lady on the beach dumped a bottle of ammonia on top of me, so I not only hurt, I stank. I could have been scarred for life. Actually, I *was* scarred for life with a burn mark across one knee. Who gives a damn how long Betty and Mike gossiped into the night?

*February 24, 1953: Ironing, ironing, etc! Ma & Phyllis both came for supper. I took Linda for a filling at the dentist. She was miserable acting.* Nice day. Nice day? *Nice day??* For Christ sake, the dentist was a scary old monster who clamped your mouth wide open then hummed Ama Pola, My Pretty Little Poppy the entire time he glared down your gullet. And she says *I* was miserable. I suppose if she manifested a certain laissez-faire approach to mothering, it is because I am a second child. There would have been more teeth gnashing if she had kept a diary when Sis was a kindergartner. And in fairness, on the rare occasion that both Sis and I managed to behave, it made headline news.

*March 5, 1952 – Went shopping this a.m. Linda & I visited Frances F. this p.m. Tonite we all tore off to Wayne & saw "Distant Drums." It was real good – so were the kids.*

# A KISS

After months of bad news and politics, I decided to tackle a more important subject: KISSING! You have your Louis Armstrong *'kiss to build a dream on'* and your Casablanca *'kiss is just a kiss,'* and what the heck is the difference? Here's my take on it.

I went to high school and college in the sixties. It was a rocking time of revolution in many major areas. Like kissing. For the first time, guys weren't the only ones allowed to 'play the field.' *Nice* girls did, too. A kiss was not saved for a one and only … you smooched several before winnowing down to the serious contenders. Yes, folks, I admit: I kissed around.

The mechanics of kissing haven't changed, even if the meaning has. Your first kiss was unlikely to have been a kiss to build a dream on. That kind of kiss takes the right time, the right place, the right (or maybe wrong) person. Nope. Your first kiss was probably on your doorstep, just before your mom screamed, "What's going on out there?" It was tentative and awkward. You were far more worried about clashing glasses or deadly breath than about whether the kiss was enjoyable or not.

Improving one's kissing technique was the first nightmove you practiced. Either I was a slow study, or it took the boy involved a longish while to manage a smacker that blew the headband right out of my hair. If the sixties did anything, it taught us that kissing was an act unto itself, not necessarily a prelude to other body parts involved in serious wildfire. Being a master of one had little to do with the other.

Cut to many decades later. I was in a conversation yesterday with three young adults (virtually all adults are younger than me). Kissing came up. All three respondents in this exhaustive research study agreed that kissing is fairly selective once more.

Has kissing become a serious commitment again? On a health level, this makes sense; my generation practiced mouth-to-mouth in the years before things like AIDS terrified us ... or before masks became yet another article of clothing to contend with. Smoochers may have wised up along the way, no longer viewing kisses as something you hand out at fairs for a buck a pucker.

Maybe you believe kissing is an act of intimacy filled with breathy promise and commitment. You know, a kiss to build a dream on. Or maybe you are an explorer. You know, a kiss is just a kiss. All I know for sure is that the rules of kissing may change, but fast or slow, commitment or no, thank heaven we continue to play the game.

# CHARMED

When people recall their childhoods, they often use diaries if their own memories are dependable as sieves. Or photo albums, of course. Some people collect a wrinkle for every worry or a battle scar for each fight over the car keys on Saturday nights.

I collected charms on a silver bracelet. I liked to hold them in my hand, feel the memories in them. I don't know if the present generation of girls gathers these little mementos symbolizing every place she goes, or anything she wants to be, or any pet she ever owned.

A Sterling silver collie charm represents my first dog and oh! how beloved she was. A downhill skier has fewer bruises than I ever had from the sport. There's the silver trumpet from my high school band days. A Hawaiian pineapple, a Williamsburg carriage, an Alaskan totem pole, a sewing machine for an art I never mastered.

A lifetime in silver.

I recently decided it was time to 'thin the herd' in my jewelry box, the one that belonged to my mother many years ago. This is a chore I haven't done in years, make that decades. And there it was: this little puddle of silver at the bottom of the chaos. It sparkled still. A woodland cabin, camping trailer, Gettysburg canon. A galloping horse, Blue Beard's Castle, an art pallet, SLR camera, Mackinac Bridge, San Francisco cable car, Glacier grizzly. Each tiny bit of metal brings a smile and a nice fat memory to run around my brain.

If I had kept collecting into my adulthood, what more would the bracelet links have to hold? Certainly, a Michigan State Spartan. A Chicago pizza slice. Maybe a martini glass. A book to represent my writing, a Washington apple, more places I've seen around the world, many more dogs, and a typewriter for my husband.

So. What to do with this item, recollections on a chain? I don't have a daughter, and I won't burden my niece with it (literally...all these charms are pretty heavy). I could sell it for scrap, but sterling is not much of an investment these days.

There is only one person in the world who finds any value in this old banjo charm, or the faith, hope, and charity trio, or the graduation mortar board. I think I will keep these little recollections in the place where valuables belong. I will carefully put my past back in the box, close the lid, and hope the next person who opens it will feel a fleeting bit of the life it holds dear.

# WILL YOU LOOK AT THAT!

As I write this, I am two days post-cataract surgery. To write it at all, I am dictating to my sister. Nothing will be the same in a few days when the *Gazette* hits your doorstep, so please take this column with a grain of salt (whatever the hell that means ... take it with a teaspoon of sugar for all I care). Think of it as fake news if you wish.

First, and I am not proud of this, I instantly fell head over heels for the surgeon. Whether this is transference or Stockholm Syndrome I do not know. The lobby in his building is filled with elderly women who haven't had this kind of feeling since Elvis demonstrated what can be done with male hips. No wonder the medical team checks your blood pressure so often.

Immediately after surgery, a sweet young thing informed me I would not be able to wear make-up for a week. Well, hell, there's a downer. I haven't been able to see well enough to apply make-up for ages. Last time I tried was maybe my Junior Prom. I ended up looking like a first cousin of Ronald McDonald. I believe I will be able to handle this gut wrenching development.

I bought reader glasses in advance to be prepared. Yesterday, I gave them a whirl. The Foster Grant people should NOT attach the glasses to a case and the packaging with those plastic strip dealies. *Note to FG: Your customer is buying your product because SHE CAN'T SEE CLOSE UP.* By the time I got the damn things ready to wear, I had cut the corner off the case and bent a bow of the glasses. I believe I have mentioned before that patience is not one of my virtues. And you know how everyone you know who wears readers can never find where they set them down? Yeah. That.

Unexpected Instant Results:

- My arm isn't long enough to get my wrist far enough away so I can read my watch.
- I was told that I would be surprised how many wrinkles I see. This is true. But I did not expect to see them on you. Everyone seems to have aged in the last two days.
- Through the haze, my face appears featureless and pale to me, sort of like a big round moon. I realize how much I always counted on the frames of my glasses to add verve, personality. A friend is extremely concerned that I am going to rush out and have glasses tattooed onto my mug ... think raccoon here. I doubt this is a genuine worry. If I can't do make-up for a week, I doubt they allow eye tats either.

All in all, I think this is one of the most amazing things available to us as we age: better vision. Cataract surgery brings definition back into your life. It also allows me to really mean things like I'll be SEEING you on the back nine.

# SITUATIONAL USELESSNESS

Advancing age dredges up unexpected deposits from the bottom of a ditch. Even if it comes as quite a surprise, we each have our own alligators to wrestle.

I have been 'suffering' lately from feelings of uselessness. I'm perplexed whether this is a dynamic of age...or if it's because the world has run seriously off the rails under our watch. Nobody wants to exit a world in worse shape than it was when we entered it.

At seventy-seven, I am the oldest of the baby boomers. I've charted my own course for a long time. But I admit I have no clue what to do to lift us back onto those rails. I vote, of course. Past that, I can't begin to see solutions for anything. I used to be one of the first to raise my hand with an answer, and now I raise it only to insert fork in piehole.

Useless. Ineffective. Futile. Not exactly the sentiments that make you want to sing, "Hallelujah C'mon Get Happy." But is this funk stemming from age? Or from an inability to superhero my fist into the face of villains?

It took me a long time to realize the difference between the two *does* matter. If this is one of the mudpies awaiting our individual futures due to age, well, then it is natural. I can learn to live with it in the same way I live with this *&^$#@) left knee.

But if it is Situational Uselessness, that is a less attractive item because it comes down to ego management. I need to quit battling the idea that I must rise to the top. If I can accept that, I think I can learn to live with the thought that problems are not up to me to solve. Solutions will jolly well have to come from elsewhere, and it is time I learn to enjoy that instead of resenting it. It's not up to me to shock and awe with brilliant elucidations; it is up to others.

Assuming this is about ego, I am trying to learn how to pull back on the reins. I've limited the drone of news in my head; if I can't do anything about it, I need solitary time away from it. I'm learning to watch videos of puppies without shame that it isn't a mind improving book. I'm developing a new writing skill that I do my best to keep ego-free. I try not to judge or be judged for a lack of greatness. And that is more than enough for me here on the back nine.

# THE ONE PERCENT

We are all in the One Percent, depending on what we are talking about. For instance, I am in the One Percent of Americans who has never liked *The Sound of Music*. I've neither seen an episode of *The Game of Thrones* nor did I follow *Downton Abbey* all the way to its conclusion. I am among a handful of females 70 + who watched *The Walking Dead*.

My viewing habits have nothing to do with superior or inferior. One Percent does not have to mean at the top, any more than it means at the bottom. It can be sliced out of the continuum anywhere along the line. We need to keep that in mind when it is used to imply dominance ... like with money.

In my career I have had clients in many corner offices. They were often rich, but that did not mean astute, happy, respected. It didn't stop a suicide. One client was just smart enough to know his brain functioned at about the level of a hedgehog. He had the office only because Daddy's name was on the masthead. He was one of the saddest people I ever knew. Being in The Saddest One Percent is nothing I aspire to, even though he wore alligator shoes and I wore nubuck.

I am in the One Percent so addicted to dark chocolate that I no longer care how good or bad it is for me. I am in the One Percent who think Bird when we hear Tweet. I am in that rarified few who resist the belief that Sasquatch, Roswell, and the Loch

Ness Monster have been debunked. Well, maybe this last is a bigger group than I know.

Just being on the Back Nine - a simple matter of longevity - gives you an opportunity to be in a One Percent that youngsters can't claim. I have seen every state and every ocean but one. I no longer give a crap that I am taller than the average American man, that I have no poker face whatsoever, that I can't hold my liquor or anyone else's.

What is your One Percent? Can you grow a perfect rose? Do you recognize different kinds of whales by their different kinds of spouts? Are you captain of an American curling team? Can you lift one eyebrow at a time? Wiggle your ears? Do you think the Olympics have been so riddled with scandal we should give up on the whole damn thing? Do you get your best stories from eavesdropping in restaurants (oh no, wait ... that one's mine)?

The world would be a very dull place if we each didn't have our own combo of One Percents that make us the only one such me or the only one such you. Thank goodness we don't all have to like or be like each other.

# LIFE SEGMENTS

I've been thinking about Life Segments, maybe because spring is the time for renewal. We each have our own segments; mine are my Michigan youth, Chicago career, Washington as author/poet. Each segment has its own highs and lows, globally and personally. They overlap, although are mostly distinct from each other. As you move from one Life Segment to the next, you do your best to conquer old grief as you look forward to new joy.

My husband was not a part of Segment One but a major player in Segment Two. He was an unusual sort of fellow. After all, the Simpsons' *Itchy & Scratchy Show* is produced by a cartoon character named after him.

He did not come very far with me into Segment Three. He missed a lot of bad stuff not being around for the last few years. He didn't have to mourn shootings of Gabby Gifford; children in Sandy Hook and Parkland; shoppers at Costco, Walmart, and King Sooper; worshippers at churches and a synagogue; fun seekers at a nightclub, a bar, a movie theatre, the Vegas Strip. He never suffered through Gangnam Style, or the Harry and Meghan melodrama, or heard that Robin Williams departed in a spectacularly unfunny way. He'll never know that I have disassembled his shrine to Kansas basketball, or that I don't watch March Madness anymore.

He would have loved the revived interest in opening the UFO secret files, the duets of Lady Gaga and Tony Bennett, and an iPad. I'm less sure how he'd react to Dotty, my spoiled-rotten Maltese.

When a spouse dies, a new Life Segment probably begins for you. It might be little obligations that get you through from one to the next. The kitchen still needs to be cleaned, the African violet on the window sill still needs to be watered, and the utility bill still needs to be paid. A trick I found for the long haul: I look at current events from his point of view as well as my own, even though he is long gone. We continue to agree or squabble. It keeps him part of my present.

His absence has not destroyed my future in Segment Three; it's just different than planned. I've built a life I love with the help of family and friends. In that way, I am a success at this widow stuff. This is the segment that will see me out. It's not his; it's my own. It's also the Life Segment in which most of us can express our opinions loudly and freely. We've earned that right.

## "CAN YOU HELP ME?"

Last month, I wrote about the difficulty of having to ask for help when you just can't do it anymore. It feels like a personal failure. Many of you reached out to tell me you agree.

But I did it. I asked. And it's been wonderful at a time my sister and I needed it, following the death of her partner of many years.

It turns out the ASKING is just what some folks need to feel the spirit of community. They don't know what they can do; you have to give them some hints. Then they fill their own need to be connected human beings at this time when we all so desperately need it. "Happy to help in any way – it makes me feel good," as one so succinctly put it.

My neighbor across the street is an electrician. And, I think, shy. For years we've communicated, when necessary, through his wife instead of face to face. Oh, we've nodded or said "nice day" but little else. Then someone broke our street lantern, and my knowledge of electricity ends with Edison. I asked for help from this man who spends his workdays doing major electrical projects. What a pain to have a neighbor ask him to do a project so far beneath his skill level and on his one day off. He not only replaced the lantern head with dusk-til-dawn activation; he went on to repaint the post. And then hauled thirteen bags of trash to the dump.

We had that much trash because a neighbor down the street offered to help clean out the garage (I'd rather tidy up Daniel's lion den having seen the spiders lurking behind our paint cans and sawhorses). This neighbor is a pilot and knows what to do with the arcane tools of the trade that Donna's partner left in our garage. In the process, over plane jacks and lathes and saws, the pilot and the electrician have become friends. The electrician's daughter wants to fly planes; the pilot has given her a couple flight lessons.

Our needs led to a friendship, unto the next generation of aviators. How biblical is that? And it isn't an isolated incident. The guy whose books I've edited is returning my hours of effort by moving furniture and repairing benches for us. He and the husband of a doctor friend work together like dervishes. A friendship appears to be brewing there, too.

And so many other things. The women who helped with the garage sale. The people who CAME to the garage sale. All people who are giving new lives to items that were old news to us. The ripples spread. Generosity of spirit manages to take root where it can multiply.

Shame on me for being so far into my eighth decade before I had the guts to ask, "Can you help me?" Give it a go. Somebody wants the opportunity to do just that for you. And who knows where it can lead.

# SECTION TWO

# Staycations, Vacations, Holidays

# BAD JUJU

I had the good fortune to spend time at the Chito Beach Resort, which is on the far side of Sekiu, WA. This is not a resort that soothes your body with spas and massages. It is a resort that soothes your sad and depleted spirit from the bad juju all around us.

Its trick is to use luxurious cabins in the quiet of the woods and water. Nature is a well-known elixir, of course. Its curative power surrounds you with time to reflect and restore. It allows you to stare happily at the tide rolling in, rolling out. It delights you with nothing more than a crab in a tidepool. It's an eagle sunbathing on the beach or a tiny calliope hummingbird with a bad attitude about your presence. For the great many of us who have moved to the Olympic Peninsula, nature is the balm that brought us here.

As there are only six cabins at Chito Beach, the handful of guests could hardly annoy each other. In fact, for a couple days we skulked around, not seeing anyone much closer than the gray whales that pass this way.

By the third day, we admitted that humans are most comfortable in packs or herds. We were there on the first days we could gather, in small numbers, outdoors without masks after the Covid shutdown. The hosts built a bonfire, and we all sat to chat with our faces on view; it felt darn near as revealing as a nude beach.

We were out of practice with small talk After the initial "hellos" and "where you headeds," conversation lulled. Digging any deeper was painful. Nobody wanted to talk politics, and nobody wanted to talk Covid. We are such a weary population. Soon, people stared into the fire, and I suspect we all paid silent homage to those who've lost their livelihoods and, worst, their lives in the last year.

In time, and with the help of wine, the chatter flowed. But it was subdued, without the shouts and belly laughs from the Time Before Masks. That kind of celebration may still be down the road, after each of us has a lot more campfires under our belt again.

I've come home with a little more hope that bad juju hasn't been permanently embedded into our land. We cannot lose this earth on our watch.

# ROAD TRIPS

I love to take off spontaneously. The roads less traveled, the unexpected sights, the wonder-where-this-goes. *Valeri Valera,* and all that. But after a recent three day escape to Oregon, I am kissing spontaneity good bye. I simply have a few more requirements than in the salad days of my youth.

1. Nothing in the world could make me sleep on the ground ever again. I am no longer spry enough to launch myself away from a wolf spider or banana slug paying a visit to my sleeping bag. Even without attack by nature, I'd suffer months of follow-up chiropractics from the crick in my neck when the air mattress collapsed.

2. I know all I care to know about gray water or black water. No freewheelin' RVin' for me. Road trips involve motels from now on. Either that or a travel partner who never questions my division of labors.

3. It's no longer easy to take any old motel vacancy. I have needs now that make spontaneity so yesterday. Does the motel take AARP or AAA? Offer frequent flyer miles? Have a bed with fewer than 100,000 miles on it? Include free shampoo, conditioner, body lotion, WIFI, cable, seriously good coffee and breakfast? Are someone else's toenail clippings caught in the carpet loops? Is there a sani-band

around the toilet seat (I know it means nothing, but it makes me feel good).

4. Speaking of toilets. I'm sorry, but no more holes in boards. Toilets need to be capable of flushing. And because many females of a certain age have exacerbated their already weak bladders by the addition of water pills, we really need them fairly often. Combine this with the fact that I have acquired a late-in-life addiction to a vanilla latte mid-morning. No matter how deep into the wilderness we plan to be, I must find the nearest town at about 10:30 am. A good travel partner never points out the obvious flaws in this plan.

I realized some while back that hiking the Pacific Crest Trail might not meet all my basic travel requirements. But after a three day "spontaneous" road trip to Oregon, I recognize matters have gotten entirely out of hand. I have become a pain in the butt even to myself.

# CRUISE CREWS

My sister and I share a love of cruising; we've been great travel partners throughout our lives. She knows my angularities, and I know hers so we rarely run into trouble when stuffed into a cabin the size of a cat kennel.

We both are eavesdroppers and people watchers (although in general, we'd rather be left alone since we don't mix well with half the population these days). We are so at ease on board when great scenery is rolling by - or when someone serves a meal the size of a brontosaurus – that we are dumbfounded to discover that others might be having a miserable time.

Following are scraps of a conversation overheard.

THE MRS to THE MR after a server has offered to bring her a free drink: "I guess we just have to get used to coffee, lemonade, or iced tea." (I wonder what other kind of free drink the poor thing has in mind ... hemlock maybe? A cup of rue?)

Turning her attention to the daily schedule of events, she mutters to THE MR, "What time's the talk on wildlife slaughter?"

THE MR. after viewing the dessert spread: "I don't want anything if it isn't lemon meringue." A harried server finds him such an item from the recesses of the ship. THE MR says: "What'd you do? Have it sent up on the dumbwaiter?"

THE MRS: "We've had two dumb waiters already today!"

The couple laughs. The server leaves.

Some people revert to babies at the drop of a diaper. Their parents do everything for them, and they still cry. For many, there's never enough. Somehow, these two self-serving jerks managed to find each other in life.

People, the old world is splitting apart in case you haven't noticed. Cruise crews don't consist of slaves anymore. Nobody rows the boat or says "Aargh" or suffers from scurvy. The food they serve isn't gross just because it isn't what you're used to at the Belly Up Buffet back home. Don't take a cruise today looking to be treated like royalty. All the crew – and most of the passengers – will want you deposed by walking the plank, or better yet, a good keel hauling on the schedule for tomorrow afternoon.

# FLATULENCE AT SEA

The sea was acting badly last night with swells of twenty feet and more. The wind slapped the ship from the side and sent wild lashings of rain and spray crashing against our balcony door. I am by and large a deep sleeper, but when you slide out of bed, well, that is a hint all is not well.

I awoke with a snort, aware that strangeness was afoot in our totally dark 176 sq. ft. cabin, which is about the size of the large popcorn bag at your local Bijou. I heard shuffling.

"Was I snoring?" I asked Sis, vaguely apologetic if I was keeping her awake, as well as vaguely concerned that the shuffling was, in point of fact, Sis.

"No," she answered. "But the room is making rude noises so I'm moving the table."

OK, I was still half asleep. Maybe I had misheard. "Huh?" I said, requesting clarification.

Almost simultaneously, I heard the sound of air being expelled through a narrow aperture from a smaller space to a larger space. Only a balloon or a Guatemalan flute or a fart is capable of this drawn out whistling sound. The kind of fart that one is trying and failing to release quietly, behind one's back as it were.

"THAT WASN'T ME," Sis pronounced in all caps to the pitch black. And I am absolutely sure that it wasn't. She is the type who would hold it in forever vs create a public mockery.

The funny thing is that she never assumed it was me, either. She hadn't awakened me to shout, "For heaven's sake, that's the last fruit buffet for you!" Instead she said, "I think it's the wind against the door. I was trying to push the table against it to stop it from shaking."

To punctuate, the room let loose with a much juicier blast, resonant and full, with the lingering echo of an M-16 set to fire in multiple bursts.

I began to giggle. Sis joined in.

"It must be the old man of the sea,' said Sis.

'Thar she blows!" said I.

"Psssfffftttssss," said the room.

It was three in the morning, in the dark, each of us in a bed as wide as a pummel horse. The sea was pounding the ship. It was scary. But we laughed until we cried while the wind forced through the door seal puffed and squealed and rat-a-tat-tatted.

God how I love to cruise.

# CRUISE UPDATE

I'm a sucker for the swell and roll of the ocean … at least from the relative safety of a cruise ship. I've just returned from such a boat ride and things aboard are changing. Here are a few hints for novice or experienced cruisers:

If a cruise company or travel agency did all your planning in the past, you need to be vigilant now. As a possible result of understaffing everywhere, I met many passengers who suffered the consequences of computer/paper/human errors. Check everything carefully before you go. And review your bill as you go to catch errors early.

Cruise companies are changing to digital communications. If you prefer paper, that's too bad … it is becoming archaic. Get to understand in advance the digital protocol of whatever cruise line you use.

About excursions: you used to be fine booking them on board. I now recommend booking them in advance. People on this cruise were not getting to places they hoped to see due to a shortage of inventory. If you don't care a lot where you tour, you'll be fine. But if you really, really want to see a certain waterfall or garden, don't wait.

Apparently, many new ships have no self-serve laundry. If you are used to doing your own, you better check with your cruise company in advance about your particular ship. You can use the ship's own laundry service, of course, but that is pretty spendy.

You will notice many little niceties now missing as cruise companies tighten their belts. Don't count on binoculars in your cabin, free lobster dinners, fresh flowers, kitchen tours, chef's parades, or mints on your pillow (this last item may be viewed as a good thing if you collapse in a drunken stupor nightly and embed those mints into your cheek).

Bigger ships mean a lot of walking just to get end to end. Many passengers rent mobility equipment which is new to them. Beware people with rental scooters … they may be out of control when trying to do complex maneuvers like reverse. We saw two shipboard accidents involving scooters and the ankles of others.

Cruise ships are moving from <u>formal</u> nights to <u>dressy</u> nights. If you don't want to pack evening gowns, then fancy tops and pants are fine. And I saw no men in tuxes other than the maître d. I guess you get to define dressy for yourselves.

There's no nice way to say this, but many people aren't nice. I observed a battle over couch pillows, for heaven's sake. As well as a table war between a mahjong team and a bridge foursome. The need to chill is the reason you took a cruise in the first place; try not to get sucked into petty feuds. And have a wonderful time.

# PINT SIZE PIRATES

I have nothing against children. I think the little germ factories should be aggressively protected, like polar bears, wolves, and fruit bats. This does not mean I want to spend a lot of time around them.

In cruise culture, Disney has catered to the young for years. If you don't cotton to bigger-than-life rodents in human clothes, you book elsewhere, and go during the school year when *those people* are occupied. This works unless you're cruising south of the equator where seasons are reversed: what you think of as the beginning of winter is actually spring break.

We stood back as 385 shrieking children boarded our ship. Cruise personnel may know how to fend off real pirates with fire hoses, but parents get fussy about that when it comes to their kids. So the cruise line surrendered the ship.

Let me divide children into two arbitrary age groups. There are the recently hatched, say under six. They run in front of old knees, finger all the rolls before choosing the one they want, and shriek out of context. But they are still at the Age of Cuteness, and the cruise staff can keep them more or less under control (probably by duct taping them to table legs when parents turn their backs).

Then there are the older kids, let's say up to fourteen. They are too old for coloring books and too young for mango tangos. Their nature says be sweet, but their hormones say raise hell. *Lord of the Flies* is an earlier account of unsupervised seafaring youth. I will be generous here and say maybe the cruise parents have not yet noticed that little Johnny is becoming a thug. Being less generous, I think Mom and Dad have figured out that if the beastie doesn't actually fall off the boat, he isn't likely to drown. So they've cut him loose. Why ruin their own vacation?

One evening, following a food fight in the buffet and a full day of elevator button Punch 'n Run, a gang of these kids took all the printer paper in the internet room, made paper airplanes and launched an airstrike of trash around the ship. They ran through the halls startling oldsters napping after a hard morning of bingo. They shuffled the pitchers of cream, skim, and whole milk and really, nobody should screw with my coffee.

But here's the thing. I'd really like to have that much fun again. The wild bunch was so rich with their own futures, so ripe with promise, so beautiful with youth, every last one of them. And I see nothing ahead for them but a distraught country, whiplashed with hate.

Now that we have decided No Child Left Behind was a bad idea, I hope we don't replace it with All Children Left Behind. Except, of course, when it comes to cruising.

# MOTEL HELL

Now that you might be quarantined for the entire length of your journey, cruising doesn't sound as much fun as it used to. I must admit, however, my worst cruise experience happened before the cruise began.

Sis and I flew to Fort Lauderdale during spring break. We arrived at midnight along with a jillion college kids who were looking for the nearest wet t-shirt contest. Sis and I, on the other hand, planned to overnight at a hotel, then escape via cruise ship the next day.

Midnight at the airport, right? The hotel lost our reservation. There were no vacancies to be had, not even with all those kids on the beach. Sis suggested to the one cruise employee we could locate, "Find us a room or your Floridian chads will be dangling from the traffic control tower."

Turns out Cruise Guy had a list of hovels for just such an emergency. He found us a vacancy. I wasn't naïve about this. I knew it wouldn't be pretty. But it was just one night. We caught a cab outside the airport. The cabbie swore in words that made even a potty mouth like me blush. Apparently, the neighborhood was not one you frequent unless armed with bazookas. Nonetheless, he dropped us in front of the motel and fled.

How many 1940s detective books have you read? Or film noirs have you seen? This was the prototype motel for every one of them: the neon sign buzzing, the ice machine humming, the slowly circulating fan, the fat lady at the desk.

We're in our blingy cruise garb.

"Want that Manny helps with the luggage? I'll go unleash him," said the lady.

"Good grief, no! Not Manny! Not at 1 am! Wouldn't want to be a bother. We'll haul our own bags, thank you kindly," said I.

We lugged everything up the stairs and into the room. Then we were faced with the problem of where to put stuff. Neither of us wanted to set anything on the carpet. The room had no glasses, no ice bucket. There was no toilet paper, not even a toilet paper holder. There *were* plenty of toe nail clippings lying about.

We stripped the beds of anything likely touched by the hourly trade and lay down as stiff as stiffs, trying to draw breath in that wet, fetid Florida air. For the next five hours neither of us actually moved, hoping not to disturb anything else that might be living in that room.

The next morning we escaped to an oceanfront Marriott and pretended to be guests. We hung out until it was time to board the ship. While using the hotel's internet, I saw a roach crawl away from the vicinity of my tote bag, and scuttle on down the hall. I can't be sure, but I believe it was another guest movin' on up from the Bates Motel.

# OLD DOGS, NEW TRICKS

I had a terrific Thanksgiving. I proved to be a carving failure, however; by the time I served, the bird was literally a hot mess. It could have been a salmon if the wings weren't sort of visible. Regardless of my knife skills, it was a lovely dinner even if we no longer have a male to carry on the cut-up tradition. I hope your day was filled with a great plenty of love and laughter, as well.

I am, luckily, getting further around the back nine each year. The aches of old age accompany me on the course, of course. But I am thrilled to announce that a joy of learning does, too. I really thought we oldsters would quit *wanting* to feed our heads. And I admit I have backed off politics as too painful to digest on a daily basis. While I also admit that a snooze next to the fire is pleasant, it is certainly not fulfilling to the old beanpot. New things are as delightful now as they ever were.

For instance, I have been taking a poetry class from Peninsula College's community program. I've learned to write villanelles and pantoums. Two weeks ago, I didn't know what either was. This is a small enough Zoom group that I'd say friendships are deepening between us all. We're supportive. How nice is that? Look into community ed programs if you haven't. Take something you never thought about before. I'm considering embalming for the next field of study.

Something else new: Sis and I looked around the house and decided we have room for a renter. Maybe a traveling nurse, now that so many medical workers need a little help in that department. We thought it would be easy. But, ye gods, the amount of grunting, groaning, bickering. I am now a real estate stager, used furniture dealer, moving lady, landlady-to-be. I have been forced to actually understand the Roku-cable connection. We are developing a rental agreement now. So far we don't allow spitting on the sidewalk, the playing of disco music, or applying any kind of cutlery to the furniture. We've redone our own rooms in the process. If you squint long enough at a room you have rearranged, you can nearly convince yourself you're on vacation.

Keep learning, stay vital. I think that will be my New Year resolution. Which means useless worry about killer hornets has moved lower on my to-do list. Year-end happiness for you and yours from this tricky old dog on the back nine.

# SPOILER ALERT

I believe I have gotten in touch with my inner Grinch this Christmas season even more than usual. Not that I want to snow on your parade. If you want to nog your eggs or conspire by your fire, well, have at it. But there's a whole lot about holiday traditions that's, frankly, a wee bit beyond my grasp.

Before going further, read that headline again: SPOILER ALERT. If you have littles who read the Opinion Page, snatch this away from them. Then, for heaven's sake, find something age appropriate for them to do.

Now then. What about the holidays turns otherwise honest parents into outrageous liars? They insist a fat man burgles your house to wedge candy and trinkets in your stockings. And that Jack Frost nips your nose at will, even though it is illegal in all states to have forced familiarity with the face of another.

Performing Christmas music is at least as odd as celebrating criminal behavior. During most months, singing indoors is just fine. But in December, singers trudge door to door wassailing uncontrollably in freezing cold. This is a thinly veiled plot to enter their neighbors' homes and drink their toddy. And all you have to do to compose a holiday song is write two syllables and repeat often. If you intend to try it, keep in mind that 'Rum pum pum pum, rum pum pum pum, rum pum pum pum' and 'Fa la, la, la, la, la, la, la, la' and 'thumpety thump thump, thumpety thump thump' are already taken.

Possibly the oddest traditions of all involve our treatment of flora and fauna. At a time of year when you might expect us to be particularly loving, we do the damnedest things to our plants and animals. We string berries together, deck halls with holly, kiss under mistletoe, drag trees indoors to cover with tinsel. Now listen people. Chipmunks do not want to form trios and sing. Fido does not want a bow on his tail. Deer prefer not to prance on roofs or fly all night long. And don't get me started on how turkeys feel about what people do with stale loaves of bread.

I suspect the true meaning of Christmas is not in the age of the fruit cakes, Mommy kissing Santa or anyone else, any number of geese a-laying, or Uncle Eldon's cherry red nose which Aunt Luella tries to pass off as just another cold, year in and year out.

I hope you each discover its own special meaning for you and find peace in a world that could truly use it.

# PRIDE

I've been thinking about Pride. Not a pride of lions, or *Pride and Prejudice*, or gay pride, or Pride Dog Food. I mean the kind that a child wants from a parent. The "I am proud of you" kind.

This desire for the approbation of a parent (or other close relative) is not optional. It's standard equipment, built into the baby at birth. Something mighty bad must have happened to a kid to truly not care about her parents' approval.

Only recently have I discovered that pride is a two-way street. I want the approval of the young, too. Yep. Geezers like me need to be told they are still worth the air they breathe.

Here's an example of what I mean:

My niece is a writer, too. In her eyes, how old and irrelevant I must seem. How opinionated, how out of touch. "Poor old Aunt Linda," my niece must whisper behind my back. "Poor old crazy Aunt Linda. Maybe we'll make room in the attic for her one day."

Turns out that isn't what she thinks at all. She read my most recent manuscript and she wrote:

"I am here to tell you that you did a really, really, really great job. I admire you so much for doing the hard work to mine this creative well of yours."

Whoa! That slammed into my heart like an arrow striking the bull's-eye. I didn't even realize how much her approval mattered. Until this. This is the brass ring. She is PROUD of me.

Pride. From the old to the young, or the young to the old. One spouse to another. A sister to a brother. Everyone wants the approval of the people who matter. No words are too sappy.

Nobody can see what you are thinking. Don't assume they know. If you have a worthy thought, let it tumble right out of your pie hole. I can tell you what Nana or Grampa would like for Christmas, and it is not another purse or tie. It is an expression that you value them. If you do, say it or write it or sing it to that person who watched you grow, lived through your messings, and loves you anyway.

Blessings and gratitude to you all this holiday. I am immeasurably proud to be read by you.

# HERE WE GO AGAIN

Once again, it's that time for new resolutions. Here are two of mine that won't cause political fallout among readers right here on the first day of the year.

THIS YEAR I WILL BUY NO NEW CLOTHES.

This may result in some catastrophic combinations by spring, of course, but I've never been a fashion plate anyway. Besides, my taste lately appears to be dark as a thundercloud. My current favorite fleece features a particularly unattractive cactus with only one pale pink flower battling to bloom amidst all those spines. Doesn't take a therapist to realize that may be a cry for help. My older clothes will offer a refreshing return to color in my closet.

The only real problem I see with this boycott on newness is that it confronts my biggest addiction: shoes. The only girly thing about me is my craving for shoes. Now in my eighth decade, I no longer purchase high heels, of course (Nancy Pelosi is remarkable for many reasons but those spiky shoes take top honors). You'd think the desire for fab footwear would burn itself out eventually. But no. I have the cutest damn collection of orthopedic steppers known to woman. Even the ones without puppies printed all over the toes.

Other than potentially falling off the shoe wagon, what else might happen that would require me to buy new clothes?

- I could gain or lose a hundred pounds.
- I could continue getting shorter.
- I could have an audience with Queen Camilla.
- I could be invited to India in the summer sizzle.

Even then, I could solve some of these issues by learning tricky bits of alteration. And really, Camilla might find it refreshing to be greeted by Port Angeles Business Casual, which is high in denim and flannel content (besides, the woman is so surrounded with dysfunctional family that I doubt she'd give a tinker's dam). If I am invited to visit India in their summer, I will turn the invitation down.

THIS YEAR FALSE OPTIMISM WON'T SAVE MOTHER EARTH.

Sayings like "Keep your face to the sun, and you won't see a shadow" or "There's always a silver lining" are officially removed from my vocabulary as hogwash. Everything does not work out for the best. Staying positive does not make good things happen. Mother Earth is in deep doo-doo, and needs us all to face that stark reality and ACT. We may not save Her, but we must give it a go. Find the fight that's right for you, and put up your dukes.

I wish us all a resolved and happy New Year.

# ONLINE DATING FOR SENIORS

Since Valentine's Day will soon be upon us, I thought I'd point out that romance can still be in the air even if you are older than granite. You just have to remember how.

I became a widow after 36 years of marriage. Five years later, I joined a dating website specifically for the geezer crowd. Here is what I found.

Four decades without a date makes your skills are rusty. Don't worry. It comes back to you. You'll do fine.

Remember this is for your own good. Go with the flow. You'll discover that any site you select will ask you some asinine questions. Don't fight it or you'll never get out of the chute.

Put together your profile to reflect who you are *now*. Do you still want to zip line across the Grand Canyon or have you given up on extreme sport? Be as honest with what you say as you are with your photos.

Question your goal. Presumably, you're no longer seeking good genes for your baby. If you want a companion vs a hubby, do you really give a hoot how tall he is? This isn't high school anymore.

People on the senior sites are looking for final relationships which aren't going to be 'long term.' We've been through marriages, divorces, deaths. We're not likely to change much. Let me say that again: WE'RE NOT LIKELY TO CHANGE MUCH. Don't make a rookie mistake of thinking you can change us. You can't. If you can't handle an atheist, a libertarian, a hunter, a tree hugger, or anything else you abhor, believe me: he or she can't change and neither can you.

That said, remember your mother isn't watching anymore. It's never too late to be curious. Live a little.

Expect regional skews. The Olympic Peninsula has its own, well, oddities. One gent wanted to know if I could skin an elk. Another was more interested in canning tuna. Sexy dress for a female seems to be hip waders. This is not true if you live in, oh say, Chicago. Keep this in mind if you decide to look outside the Pacific Northwest.

Young people have their own list of watch-out-fors. So do we. Some men are looking for a nurse with a purse to take care of them when their health slips. Men have told me they are frequently approached by women seeking Sugar Daddies. I'm not saying that either is necessarily bad, just know the truth of what you're signing on for.

Bottom line, the experience has been fun. If you decide to try it, don't be a chucklehead. Don't send somebody money to buy a ticket to come see you. Don't meet in a graveyard at midnight. If you use your head as well as your heart, you just might have a great time.

# GOING THE DISTANCE

My sister ordered shampoo from Costco. It was a buy-one-get-one bargain, and we received two industrial-sized drums of the stuff. We will not have to buy shampoo again for the rest of our days.

This got me to thinking about what else I've done or purchased for the last time. Some of this is delightful, like not having to go through the car buying song-and-dance ever again. I expect my current chariot will carry me through the last of my Sunday drives. Also on the delightful side? Certain medical procedures I've aged out of; you can guess. And I haven't worried about pregnancy in years.

Some of it is sad, like knowing I won't ever get another puppy. My old dog will see me out or vice versa. Some of it is even preplanned … I chose a doctor enough younger than me to go the distance. I won't have to start over, or at least that's my theory. Some of it is obligation; we're getting the house painted this summer. Never again (have you checked the price of paint lately?).

My memories of travel are better than actual travel. There aren't enough bathrooms in the desert to make me truly comfy on long road trips anymore. Going on a cruise loses its appeal as getting on the ship means battling the other 2000 passengers, each armed with a mobility device. And OMG, a plane to fly the friendly skies? Think more in terms of the "head 'em up, move'em out" school of cattle drives.

Fortunately, I'm running out of money to travel at about the same time I'm running out of desire to travel. I've bought my last suitcase. I've also bought my last bottle of alcohol (it conflicts with my old lady pills). I'm done with artwork for my walls. I'll switch to paper plates if this dishwasher hits the bricks.

But! This doesn't mean my shopping sprees are done. The tree I plant today won't grow to shade a reunion picnic in my lifetime. But plant we must. I will continue buying books and shoes although I can't conceivably wear out the ones I've stockpiled. I'm signing up for another poetry class or two ... writing a poem doesn't take as long as writing a book, and it keeps my mind active.

I have not expressed my last opinion, made my last friend, had my last dark chocolate. These valuables I take with me right up to the brink of the great beyond.

# SECTION THREE

# Writing

# APRIL FLOWERS

April is a very busy month on the national calendar. It is Prevention of Cruelty to Animals month, Autism Acceptance month, National Frog month, Garden Month, and many, many more. Stress Awareness month is in April, too, but I feel most of us are plenty aware of stress already.

The month has celebratory weeks as well as months. Like National Parks, Earth, and Young Adult Cancer Awareness weeks. And oh, the days! Library Day, World Health Day, and believe it or not there is a special April day reserved for each of the following: rats, Siamese cats, beavers, pygmy hippos, hamsters, dolphins, elephants, bats, curlew, penguins, tapirs, and guide dogs. So you have plenty to think about in April other than spring cleaning or resurfacing the driveway.

Personally, I think April's finest flower is National Poetry Month. There is a guess that April was Shakespeare's birthday month. I doubt it. If nobody is sure what all he actually wrote, I doubt they are sure when he appeared on the scene. But I digress.

I can hear some of you saying, "Poetry? Here on the opinion page? I'll give you an opinion."

For the rest of you, know that poetry is alive and well in your own neighborhood. The Peninsula speaks to writers, so writers speak of it. Poetry is our most personal way to communicate deepest joys and fears to each other. When you read a poem that shares your feelings, you know you are not alone. March may be known for madness ... but April is known for poetry that clears the mind, offers wisdom, and shares our humanity. Give another read to Whitman's "When Lilacs Last in the Dooryard Bloom'd" or if you like a challenge, take on Eliot's "The Waste Land" which begins *April is the Cruelest Month*, or merely enjoy this sweet bit of happy from Ogden Nash:

> Praise the spells and bless the charms,
> I found April in my arms.
> April golden, April cloudy,
> Gracious, cruel, tender, rowdy;
> April soft in flowered languor,
> April cold with sudden anger,
> Ever changing, ever true --
> I love April, I love you.

There are lots of poetry readings in our community, and you will be amazed by the talent of local bards. Give a reading a try. Many art galleries host them, as do libraries, theatres, coffee shops, bars. It's an easy way to get involved locally ... even to feature your own verse.

You'll likely discover that National Poetry Month is better than gold and easier to mine. And at least as worthy of praise as bats and rats.

# WHAT TO WEAR ON A FLYING BEAR

Due to my current interest in writing poetry, I have not worked on a novel for well over a year. That's a colossal change for me, having created ten of them in the recent past.

My headful of characters is getting annoyed with me. Yes, a writer's characters DO feel free with their opinions, especially if you haven't murdered one somewhere along the way. The remaining dozens let you know their attitudes and can be quite vengeful. For instance, Will, the fictional embalmer at a funeral home, knows I spared his life only because my sister begged for it. He has some creative plans for my own demise when that time comes around. Moral: don't piss off the embalmer who has final say over how you look.

I guess this is some form of dissociation. You know how you can sometimes drive home (stone cold sober) but have no real memory of the trip until you pull in the driveway? That kind of dissociation. I appear to get through periods of conversations in my own head without letting the house burn down.

If not dissociation, this delight in making up stories is definitely a form of bearing false witness. I really must reread that Ninth Commandment a time or two.

"Bearing false witness" made my character Bear growl at me. He is a retired curmudgeon crime solver. He's never been truly happy since his mentor Andy Rooney died, and he had to settle for Bernie Sanders. He is clamoring for another book about the many crime bosses in his younger years.

The lovely Mrs. Monroe is worried I'll tell what she really did for those three months she disappeared in San Francisco, just before the big fire. She need not worry ... I don't write X-rated books, nor do I know much about arson in the early nineteen hundreds.

Frankly, with ten years of made-up people in my head, I rarely need a real person to talk with. That's a truth about writers; we can look quite alarmingly dull just sitting there. And yet, we're hard at work plotting heists or figuring out how to add details of Alaska prohibition into a tale about frontier teachers. We almost certainly are eavesdropping on your conversation in hopes of dialog to steal.

The old saw is to write what you know. Baloney. You don't have to be a murderer, a bootlegger, or a pole dancer to write about murder, alcoholism, the arts. But you have to work at it, investigate, interview, be known at historical societies, spend countless evenings online. You can write about places you've never seen, actions you've never taken, emotions you've never felt, events that will never come around again. Do the research, top it with imagination, and off you go.

Speaking of going, I must be on my way. My fantasy heroine wants something to wear other than t-shirts with bad slogans. What do you think a spirit should wear while riding her flying bear through the Pacific Northwest forest?

# FEELIN' GROOVY

I'm writing a novel that has a character named Mrs. Borg. At my writers critique group, some smart guy pointed out that in one place, I spelled it Mrs. Bong. This led to accusations regarding my use of pot.

The last time I smoked weed was also the last time I was a flower child. Both are hazy remnants of a distant youth. But recently my sister and I have become interested in the use of dope on pain. Is it true there can be relief or are you just a dope to believe it?

I am not a bold person so I circled the idea for a very long time. Then I circled the marijuana shops. I have my standards. It couldn't look like a dive. It had to have RESPECTABLE painted across its front door. It could not have words like Reefer or Doobie in its name.

The warning we saw at the door was to leave our guns outside. These days, I suppose that is not bad advice at any retailer. Or church. Or school. But I would have preferred a welcome mat. The shop was very clean, neat and friendly. No roaches ... of any kind.

The first person Sis and I met was the customer in line ahead of us. He said his name was 'Squatch, and he looked like the real McCoy. Even without one hit, I was already hallucinating.

Next we noticed that marijuana has become a brand name business. In my day there was only Maui Wowie and Acapulco Gold. Not anymore. Dozens of names, strengths, delivery systems each with actual ADVERTISING. Posters and pamphlets. Strengths and flavors. Had I known, I would have dragged in our camp chairs for a sit-down label reading session. Instead, a lovely clerk took us aside, easily identifying us as newbies. She was gentle. And kind. Asked our needs. Then broke into gibberish.

"High CBD?"

"Ah ..."

"THC?"

"Ah ..."

"Both?"

"Ah ..."

"Capsule, tincture, gel, sublingual?"

Well, you get the idea. Decisions. Our recommended products were Flow, Relief and Happiest Self. Gotta say, the MJ folks have it all over the Pharma folks when it comes to comforting med names.

Does it work? Time will tell. Maybe it won't stop insomnia but will stop your anxiety about insomnia. The ointment probably won't solve pain but might offer a nice warm release to joints (the kind in your body, not in your hand).

If you've been thinking of hauling your old crate into a shop, give it a go. Talk to a doctor or a physical therapist beforehand to feel more secure, but you will find lots of other geezers in there so you won't feel alone. Just be aware it ain't Costco: there are no free samples.

# CREATIVE SPARKS

The reason it is difficult to research facts about creative people is that they are creative people. Personality profiles can only go so far when the test subject's brain is in any one of a dozen locations at the time. Sound like Dissociative Identity Disorder? Well, maybe, sort of.

Many years ago a research project was done by a chain of art stores in Chicago. I have long since forgotten the actual numbers, but they found something like 90% of children think of themselves as artists, while under 10% of adults do.

How sad is that?

It gets driven out of you, primarily by a need to make a living. Only a tiny percentage of creative folk can live on their art alone. The magical reality inhabited by creators of music or paintings or words - that territory so fertile for the imaginative brain - has very little to do with feeding the kiddies and kitties. Then add a second pie-in-the-face in the disgruntling form of living today and, well, flights of fancy are easily trampled.

Or maybe not. Creativity comes back to life in the senior years for many people. That is an established fact. Elders have time, and maybe, just maybe, they have wisdom. But I think that I would now add that creativity abounds "during the adverse conditions of lockdown" regardless of age. I have recently become aware of some astounding work being done by writers in our community. I am a co-founder of a group called Olympic Peninsula Authors; we have just closed the submissions for our upcoming anthology about prevailing in times like these.

We have been amazed by the number of submissions. Of course, we expected to hear from several beloved local authors, and we have. What gobsmacked us is the number of submissions from people we don't know. People are using the Age of Covid, Fire, and Fury to write. Memoirs, poetry, essays, rants, romance so hot it burns your hands to flip the pages. I assume increased activity is alive among composers and sculptors as well.

So what does this mean? I don't know. Maybe it's the same thing that makes an endangered songbird still express its heart. Maybe most of us have the need to stoke what embers remain in our souls. Maybe it means nothing at all but a wounded cry in the wilderness.

I don't know. But what I *do* know is that the creative spirit is burning bright, irrepressibly so. I hope it is thriving for you.

# SECTION FOUR

## This and That

# CHIP SHOTS ONE

If you've read this column before, you know that *View from the Back Nine* has more to do with old age than with smacking a ball. Nonetheless, in keeping with golfy imagery, I call the following short subjects Chip Shots.

**I have a new chair.** I can see why you may think this is not exactly newsworthy, but it is to me. The owner was a tiny little lady not up to a Battle with the Beast. This is how I was gifted this nearly new $1500 chair, something I had never aspired to.

Do you have any idea the technology that has gone into recliners? The last one I purchased was about the same time the Bears were doing the Super Bowl Shuffle, so I had no idea what has gone on since.

This thing is as complex as a mechanical bull. It is the ONLY chair I have ever owned that came with detailed instructions for usage (usually the instructions are *back yourself up and sit*). Maybe it's so complex because it doubles as a full-length bed and an elevator. Nothing else in the house is so loaded with emergency preparedness. It has back up batteries for when the power goes out so that you can get out of it since there is no manual overdrive.

The day will come that I will need the 'ejection assist' it is armed with. For now, I can't get out of it until it is good and ready. Which is quite a learning experience when you are used to getting to the phone before it stops ringing.

**It is nearly time for the Sequim Farmers and Artisans Market.** My friend Heidi and I run a booth selling books by local authors. Since it is a not-for-profit, we do everything on a shoestring. But this year we bought a new booth. Not white, like all the others. Ours is purple- striped. *Garish* might be an accurate descriptive of the decor. We'll see how many infractions of the rules we are committing. If you see two elderly women sitting out there with no booth whatsoever, you'll know we're in the penalty box.

**Sis and I have a hot tub that hasn't been used in forever.** We're getting it up and running again since it will be our staycation. Part of the revitalizing process is to shock your hot tub. Turns out this doesn't mean to let it see you in your bathing suit. It involves the addition of forty chemicals, an incantation by a deranged priest, and planting a potato in the back yard. We'll see how it goes.

# CHIP SHOTS TWO

It's too hot for sustained thought. So here are a few random reflections flickering through my mind this August.

**I had an EKG the other day,** and the youthful technician warned me that the removal of the stickers from my legs might feel like a mini-wax. I told her the gold in the golden years is that leg hair mostly disappears. She seemed thrilled to know that. And then I explained all the other things that disappear.

**Sis and I have a new rescue dog named Jinx.** Jinx will go down the outdoor steps only if our other dog leads the way. And she won't come up them although we've tried negotiations, peace talks, cease fires, treats, and threats. So one of us clambers down the steps to open the lower door to allow Jinx to come through the garage and into the house. She's done a really fine job training us, don't you think?

**I don't want to learn any more computer programs.** If I can't do it now, it doesn't matter to me. I will be depending on the kindness of others. You have been warned.

**Have you noticed an increase in butterflies this summer?** I've seen more swallowtails in my yard than I have for a long time. Thanks to all you careful gardeners. Your efforts are showing off bright yellow in the sun.

**I've spent eight decades with binary pronouns.** Don't expect me to be a quick-change artist. I'm having to measure your needs against my belief that plural pronouns don't belong with singular subjects. I am making the effort, but the shift is happening at the speed glaciers used to go years ago.

**Speaking of euphemisms.** When a restaurant says 'field greens' it means 'weeds.' I don't want weeds in my salads. Gimme iceberg or romaine or leaf and leave the rest of that stuff out with the cowpies where it belongs.

**I haven't worn makeup in years.** But I've been invited to a wedding, and since I'd rather not go as Mother Time, I thought I'd try a few cosmetics. I rummaged in the back of my dresser drawers and unearthed pencils and jars that haven't seen the light of day since the Jurassic Era. I applied the items that had not totally crusted over. If I go to the wedding like this, people will think I am the specter of Clarabell, returned from the dead.

# CHIP SHOTS THREE

**Rainier cherries are appearing in grocery stores again.** They always remind me of a flight I took to Georgia to visit a client. I carried along a big container of cherries to put in the center of the conference room table. The Georgians back then had never had such cherries. They gathered like squirrels. They taste tested, beamed, and dug in. They forgot all about peaches. One gentleman, during a break, distributed his cherry pits to the place settings of the others; he didn't want anyone to know how many cherries he had eaten. It was a very successful meeting. I learned right then that "getting to any heart through the stomach" is an absolute truth in life.

**To all you new June brides,** I hope your wedding was less exciting than the one described in a Letter to the Editor that ran in my hometown paper, over half a century ago:

Our Apologies....

To all of the wonderful friends and relatives who attended the Smith wedding and reception in Germfask on Friday, November 5th. The language, attire and general behavior of the groom thoroughly offended and shamed us all.

We wish to thank the State Police and ambulance drivers from Manistique for their prompt arrival, even though we were disappointed that no arrest was made.

We are pleased that our wife and mother was released from the hospital and is recuperating at home with only a broken arm.

Again we say we are sorry and shamed by the action of the man our daughter and sister chose.

**These days, we use the trade speak of mental health** to pick on each other a trifle too freely. CNN recently warned of this, and I agree. Not everybody is on the spectrum. Are you really depressed or merely sad? "I gray rocked the narcissist who's breadcrumbing me" may sound like I am a hipster with my thumb on the heartbeat of modern issues, but mostly it's proof I don't have the sense God gave a goose. Before we throw terms around, it's probably a good idea to seek definitions from the brainiacs who invented them to describe issues more serious than computer dating.

# LONELINESS

I see this horse every other Wednesday when I'm on my way to my writer's critique group. He is not close to the road; a large field of lavender separates me from his pasture. Consequently, I do not speak to him or give him carrots. I wouldn't offer food anyway without an owner's okay. I play by the rules in most things.

This horse has fascinated me for many months. He is no magnificent stallion, racing the wind. He is not even particularly handsome what with his Roman nose. Nevertheless, he has a flowing whip of a tail and a graceful arch to his neck like most of his kind. His rotund girth might be a sign he has an ability to fend for himself. Or not.

He fascinates me because I believe he is sad. He is a herd animal, after all, and here he is all on his own, and that is the type of thing that can make me sad for days. You might say I am a patsy unless you are snarky enough to call me a chump. Anyway, he stands at the fence, facing across the fields, staring at the dairy cows acres away. That's how I always see him. He whinnies to them, but they ignore him because they have milk to make. I'm sure he must have a human somewhere, but I have never seen this person.

Some goddess of lonely horses took pity on him a few weeks back, and I noticed that a sleek little bay had been released in the pasture with him. I was thrilled and pulled off the road just to watch the magic of new friendship. Imagine my chagrin when the two knuckleheads bucked along the fence line, ears back, lashing at each other with hooves and teeth. I am no horse whisperer, but it appeared they were not having fun. Further, it appeared that my horse was the aggressor nation. The next week, he was alone again, looking over the fence with longing and sorrow, or so it seemed to me.

This week, the horse goddess devised another plan. Goats are in the pasture. They are eating. And the horse is calmly grazing as well, close to the little animals' sides. If I were Aesop, I'd find some moral here. Maybe that opposites attract, or that loners like to be alone, or that everyone who looks like a friend might not be, or that it takes all kinds. Mostly, though, I just feel better because the horse seems content with his goats.

As for now, this ending is a happy one.

# WILL YOU LOOK AT THAT!

As I write this, I am two days post-cataract surgery. To write it at all, I am dictating to my sister. Nothing will be the same in a few days when the *Gazette* hits your mailbox, so please take this column with a grain of salt (whatever the hell that means ... take it with a teaspoon of sugar for all I care). Think of it as fake news if you wish.

First, and I am not proud of this, I instantly fall head over heels for the handsome surgeon. Whether this is transference or Stockholm Syndrome I do not know. The lobby in his building is filled with elderly women who haven't had these kind of feelings since Elvis demonstrated what can be done with male hips. No wonder the medical team checks your blood pressure so often.

Immediately after surgery,  a sweet young thing informs me I will not be able to wear make-up for a week. Well, hell, there's a downer. I haven't been able to see well enough to apply make-up for ages. Last time I tried was maybe my Junior Prom. I ended up looking like a first cousin of Ronald McDonald. I believe I will be able to handle this gut wrenching development.

I bought reader glasses in advance to be prepared. Yesterday, I gave them a whirl. The Foster Grant people should NOT attach the glasses to a case and the packaging with those plastic strip dealies. *Note to FG: Your customer is buying your product because SHE CAN'T SEE CLOSE UP.* By the time I got the damn things ready to wear, I had cut the corner off the case and bent a bow of the glasses. I believe I have mentioned before that patience is not one of my virtues. And you know how everyone you know who wears readers can never find where they set them down? Yeah. That.

Unexpected Instant Results:

My arm isn't long enough to get my wrist far enough away so I can read my watch.

I was told that I would be surprised how many wrinkles I see. This is true. But I did not expect to see them on you. Everyone seems to have aged in the last two days.

Through the haze, my face appears featureless and pale to me, sort of like a big round moon. I realize how much I always counted on the frames of my glasses to add verve, personality. A friend is extremely concerned that I am going to rush out and have glasses tattooed onto my mug ... think raccoon here. I doubt this is a genuine worry. If I can't do make-up for a week, I doubt they allow eye tats either.

All in all, I think this is one of the most amazing things available to us as we age: better vision. Cataract surgery brings definition back into your life. It also allows me to really mean things like I'll be SEEING you on the back nine.

# THREE STRIKES

It's been a trifecta sort of day.

The dishwasher stopped working and leaked water which seeped under the floorboards.

Sis's computer quit making any kind of sound.

The battery in our oldest fliver went flopbot.

The last time the battery needed a jump, we called our emergency road service, and the guy who came out looked very concerned when he regarded the two of us. He proceeded to lecture us about getting a battery charger. It felt like a scene out of THELMA AND LOUISE ACTUALLY SURVIVED AND GOT TOO OLD TO BE TRUSTED ON THEIR OWN.

We did subsequently purchase a battery charger. But we couldn't get it to work which is largely due to instructions that were translated out of some language into some other one, neither bearing a resemblance to any language we recognize.

However, we didn't want to call the road serviced guy again because we didn't want to concern him unduly. Oh, that's rot: we didn't want another lecture. We had to fix it. Sis succeeded when our renter took pity on his elderly landladies huddling next to the dead car in the driveway. He got it working. Really, it is terribly unfortunate how our dog treated him assuming he was up to no good.

The dishwasher is past its use-by date by a few dozen years so the fact it needs a burial is no big mystery. What to do about the curling floor boards, now that's the mystery. Meanwhile, Sis totaled the price of a new machine, delivery, haulage of old machine, installation of new machine, and you know what? We both remembered we at one time knew how to wash dishes by hand! Mom taught us during the Iron Age.

Regarding the computer sound issue? Well, for this one day, it's nice not to be shrieked at by politicos. Like Scarlet, I'll think about that tomorrow. Guess we'll get out our trumpet and tonette for an evening of home entertainment.

A day like this is miserable for anyone living alone. Living alone takes so much work. If you don't do it, it doesn't get done. Since I don't live alone (in case you're wondering, Sis and I are both widows and share a house), we can deal with online searches and phone calls and pleading with service people. We have plenty of time to do that and still get back to worrying about how long the water heater will last.

# ACRONRYMS SAY IT ALL

Everything today is a syndrome, a condition, a dysfunction. RLS, STD, IBS, GAD. You get the idea (BTW, the language of texting hasn't helped with RAS, Ridiculous Acronym Syndrome). Some acronyms punctuate very serious problems; these are not the ones I'm addressing here so please don't complain, because I don't RSVP to FAQs unless they are SWAK. I'm just saying.

I'm talking here about those acronyms that are disorders of the hour. You can feel rather left out if you don't have your own acronym to discuss at the next cocktail party (should we ever again be allowed to gather within a three foot distance of each other).

I thought I would come up with a few suggestions that you are welcome to use, for reasons of your own. Let's face it. It's a lot easier to say you have PYND than to admit that your disorder is Picking Your Nose. I hasten to add that the WHO or CDC have not officially recognized the following conditions.

DDD is a common dysfunction for those who mysteriously disappear when it's time to clear the table. Dishpan Diarrhea Disorder is particularly widespread in households with teens.

Do you feel warn down? Enjoy a good sulk? My Aunt Mary would say you suffer SOMS or Suck On The Mop Syndrome. This situational depression is largely related to viewing too much news.

JASS is so pervasive we all have a friend or spouse who suffers it. Just A Second Syndrome has no known cure, affecting those who have it with chronic lateness and wastage of others' time. It results in a corresponding condition known as IAS, Irritated Acquaintance Syndrome.

The best treatment for PMS is to Purchase More Shoes...you are a MORC if your Middle of the Road Condition makes you a bore...if you often put your foot in it, you no doubt suffer IBM or Irritating Big Mouth.

Several new disorders were fallout from Covid-19, or SIPI, Shelter In Place Isolation. Four of the most generally recognized were:

NTST (No Televised Sports Trauma)

GLOLS (Grumpy Little Old Lady Syndrome)

AWGD (Accelerated Weight Gain Depression)

TLPSH (This Little Piggy Stayed Home)

Fortunately, this bundle has pretty much been put on a top shelf. Except AWGD. That bitch is here to stay.

# AND THE WINNER IS . . .

This "opinion piece" will run the day after the election of 2020; I am writing it two days before. You'll already know what I do not.

Truman was President when I was born, but I don't remember him, and I'm pretty sure he doesn't remember me. I liked Ike and even admired that upstart boy and his family in Camelot. Next came the beagle ear-puller, then the "your president is not a crook" crook, and his replacement who proclaimed that the long national nightmare was over. We must have been in great need of kindness to have elected Carter and completely devil-may-care when we turned to Hollywood for a leader. The Bushes, Clinton, Obama, Trump . . . well you remember them all and their foibles.

So I have been through quite a few of these four-year bloodbaths. I'll admit this one feels like the Super Bowl of all elections. Will - or should I say did - Budweiser and Apple and Pepsi wow us with commercials on the big day (yesterday)? It's a big day not only for who wins, but for what it says about us. You and me. Will we hate each other or hold out a glove-covered hand? How deeply does the fault lie in ourselves instead of the stars?

Maybe the human species has gone as far as it can go. This Big Blue Marble is in a helluva mess. AI is less scary than the faulty old programs that made our own brains functional ... we seem to have passed their use-by date. Maybe it's time for newly evolved adams and eves, models with face flaps and no need for water and little fear of change. If they fear change these days, they'd never leave the garden, and what help would that be?

Our problems were monumental long before COVID-19. On the downside, none of us can leave the country if we hate the election results; on the upside, this stay-at-home time helps us bring neighbors together. Mine are purchasing a sno-blower together to meet the coming winter. I consider this positive since it implies there will *be* a coming winter.

Today, the day after the election, you will be feeling a little more hope or a little more despair, depending on how the wind blows for your candidates. Whether depressed or joyful, give each other a little room. Don't be a knee-jerk jerk. Both sides are capable of acting like nincompoops; I know that, because I have been one myself. Walk away from confrontation. There will be plenty of time for that. Instead, use a little time to consider what the hell are we going to do next?

# EMOTIONAL DEBT

The debt limit deal is done, for better or worse. The haggling and hissing will continue ad infinitum. So it goes.

Meanwhile, I've been thinking about the other kind of debt limit we all juggle – let's call it Emotional Debt. It is a very hard time for many of us who are used to some basic niceties. Easily available health care (just try to find a doctor). A living space that doesn't cost more than we make. Enough food so everyone eats.

I think of Emotional Debt as a bag of gold nuggets. The whole idea is simple: nuggets in and nuggets out to maintain some kind of balance between happiness, love, anger, hate. Right now, those base emotions are on the rise.

Living in this fractious world is no piece of cake. Do you huddle at home and always wear a mask when you must rabbit outside for a fresh load of carrots? Or do you accept that virus is a part of our life like auto accidents or computer hackers or Cascadia rising – dangers we learn to live with and go on as best we can. Should we put ourselves or our clan first or exhaust ourselves trying to answer to both?

The intensity of Emotional Debt is higher than ever. Maybe it is merely a biproduct of my own age (Methuselah comes to mind) that I know so many people living tough with unanswerable problems that are tearing them apart. Problems that leave me feeling helpless. Bad moon on the rise.

The thing stripping away my emotional nuggets is the constant hate and hopelessness. We seethe with the injustice of it all. I am upset so much of the time that eating dessert first is no longer a joke – it makes sense with so little time between calamities.

In 1867, Matthew Arnold wrote these final words to Dover Beach:

> *And we are here as on a darkling plain*
> *Swept with confused alarms of struggle and flight,*
> *Where ignorant armies clash by night.*

Strife isn't new. It appears to be part of the human condition to destroy, and we refuse to let history teach us much at all. Hope for our future must come from the future, not the past. Survival is up to fresh young faces. Meanwhile, I find myself turning inward to my local life to refill Emotional Debt with joy or laughter or empathy. Here such things can still exist and will sustain me until the bell tolls.

# WHO SHARES YOUR TRUTHS?

If I had been born one year earlier, I would have been the last of the Silent Generation instead of the earliest Baby Boomer. I guess that makes me a traditionalist with a rebellious streak. I was raised knowing that to tell the truth was a good thing unless it was personal, in which case it was TMI, a mishap without a name back then, but it existed all the same.

Who do you share your truths with? Elmo? Your pet, a spouse, a best friend, a total stranger who drove your Uber or cut your hair or served you a drink? Who knows your ugliest thoughts as well as your best intentions? One thing that aging has taught me is that we might all be better off if we DID share more of our truths and worry less about privacy which has, after all, become a lost commodity.

I have found truth in other old women, those of us from the first generation in which women were educated by the millions. From the generation whose parents fought tooth-and-nail to provide for daughters as well as sons. From the first generation that believed a Barbie could be a pilot or a brain surgeon, then set out to prove it.

I find amazing truths from these women in their seventies and beyond. If there is any wisdom left on earth, you will find it here. We fought to remove the word "chattel" from divorce papers and to retain our own credit ratings even if the Mister's sucked.

We fought for birth control. We fought glass ceilings and are terrified once again that the cracks will close on our younger sisters.

These women have found ways to deal with their problems and have lived with them for decades. They've survived abuse or domination, they've walked the walk, not just crying fowl but doing something about it. They're problem solvers because they've had to be. They've been participants and are now observers, with great insight to share with anyone who might choose to listen. I suspect this is why so many older women are poets: poetry by its very nature confronts things that are easier to kick under the rug.

Older women carry truths for each other. It's where I choose to face down my ghosts with old lady Sally or Claudia or Betty Jo Jean. It is a marvelous age with lots to share, politics to babies. These women have handled grief and sorrow; they can handle yours as well.

These women are the gold in the golden years.

# SECTION FIVE

# People on my Path

# MESSING WITH MOTHER NATURE

I know a young couple who created a glorious garden together. In addition to veggies (including an annoying amount of zucchini) and flowers, they've planted grafted trees, surrounding them well with doe-defying wire.

The grafted apple tree is a marvel to me. Its slender branches wrestle with Gravenstein, honey crisp, cosmic and something else I forgot. NOTE: I am not an agrarian expert nor is my memory what it used to be, so you may have to lower your standards a bit and agree that close is close enough.

What's important is that the couple knows exactly which variety will be a pie, which will make an applesauce, which is best to bob for, and which is juicy lusciousness eaten there in the orchard, picked right off the tree. They are ready to pounce as the apple varieties appear, synchronized as a SWAT team. The same can be said for their collection technique of Santa Rosas, Italians, and Black Rubies on their plum tree.

Across town and slightly up the mountainside, I have another friend whose hair is whiter and who might be a little wiser. Or not. Age is no guarantee that we've learned a damn thing.

Whatever, she certainly knows a bargain. She purchased a grafted pear tree at a deep discount because the store lost the ticket with the list of pears the tree would produce. She delights in her nameless pears, be they Bartlett, bosc, or comice. I've asked her to report to me if she actually finds any partridges amid the pears as she gathers her harvest each autumn. So far that reported association between partridge and pear has been debunked by empirical evidence.

I realize some of you may think all this fruit grafting could be too much mucking about with Science, just like it was when Vincent Price bonded – literally - with that fly. Maybe the "plant a turnip, get a turnip" school of thought should be good enough for us all. We're already doing enough to make Mother Nature plenty mad at our wicked ways.

I'm sure some point could be made here about how we can all succeed nurtured by the same root stock. Or maybe just a universal gladness for the life force of trees, like the Maui banyan showing signs of regrowth.

In the meantime, if I'm offered it, I'm accepting a tub of that apple sauce or slice of pear pie. If not offered, I'll be forced to contemplate theft which is the only real forbidden fruit of gardening. It will never happen though … the deer would beat me to it.

# LIVE AND LEARN

A fourteen-year-old boy posted a notice asking if people had chores he could do. Sis and I needed to have weeds pulled so she called him. The negotiation was highly professional. Since he didn't know us, he would bring along his sixteen-year-old brother. And his mom would drive them here and back. Sis hired him.

I'm sure the iffy economics of this situation (his overhead of payback promises must be enormous) will cause his business to flag before the autumn is out. I will never know for sure because, highly professionally, he fired us.

"You have too many spiders in your yard," he said. "I won't be back."

Too many spiders?

Apparently, the arachnid population is out of hand. Frankly, I am not aware of roaming bands of eight leggers infesting in the backyard. And I WOULD be aware since I suffer a bit from this particular phobia myself. Which may be why I'm not the one out there weeding.

This all leads me to think the young lad might want to hone down his list of available services using some common sense. Hate snakes? Don't watch *Snakes on a Plane*. Have a thing about showers? Don't watch *Psycho*. Scared of spiders? Don't do yardwork. I'm just saying.

But that is a bit harsh. Maybe he's honing as we speak. Any of us who have started a business know you find yourself doing tasks you never dreamed of. When you open your office, you are likely to be the one cleaning the carpets because you will not have a janitorial department. Installing the locks because you will not have a security department. Learning to keep books because you will not have an accounting department. Dealing with HR issues because you will not have an HR department. None of this has anything to do with your skills as a dentist or masseuse or public relationships expert. But it has everything to do with keeping the bill collector from the door.

Or maybe I should say keeping the spiders from the door. I give this young businessman credit for doing the job he was hired to do before deciding he wouldn't be back. For having the courage to tell us why. For having the ambition to start his enterprise. He'll live and learn. And I figure, he'll end up doing it well. Thanks to a caring Mom and a very obliging big brother for getting him up and running.

# MR. FUDGE V. THE CUPCAKE COUPLE

To sell my books, I often attend Arts & Crafts shows. There are basically two types; some are local with 'juried' artisans. My experience is that these vendors are a pretty terrific group with carefully made products.

Then you have the big shows, the ones with vendors on regional - or even national - circuits. Think state fairs or larger. If not big business, it's certainly biggish business. At these shows, it's easier to get trampled to death in the craft hall than the horse barn.

My first experience with a show this size was a three-day marathon. I watched, mouth agape, as vendors arrived with monster RVs like NASCAR teams or rock bands, names emblazoned along the sides of their rigs. Fifth wheels, custom vans, motor homes. They took over all the spaces at the nearest state park.

Some are pros. But many are retired couples, maybe one making metal sea creatures and the other bracelets from old spoons. They travel between shows during the week, seeing the sights, living comfortably in their RVs. Then they set up a display Fridays, Saturdays, and Sundays from May through December. They've found a way to cover the cost of travel while they tour the country. They are the modern day extension of the carnies of yesteryear.

I felt like a rube at my first show of this size. Sis and I arrived in a twelve-year-old RAV with Rubbermaid tubs full of books. There we were with a booth approximately as sophisticated as Lucy's nickel psychological advice stand.

As we set up, I was amazed at vendors fighting for their 'rights' like hummingbirds at a feeder. Nobody gave one single inch to the vendor next to them. I was asked to take sides against Cat Lady by Metal Man and complain about the scented candles conflicting with the soap aromas.

If I had known what I was doing, I might have whined about my booth space. For unknown reasons, the show organizers placed us between Mr. Fudge and Cupcake Couple. Three days captured between delectables; what a horror show, right? As it turned out, it was. They bickered over our heads throughout the event.

"If you give so many free samples nobody will buy anything!"

"At least I'm not too ashamed of my products to offer samples."

You get the idea. After the first day of that, even fudge stopped sounding yummy.

As a writer I was fascinated by this new-to-me lifestyle of seniors on the road. This was primary research, by golly, at its rawest. So, of course, I wrote a story about a murder at a craft show. I'll be ready for the circuit next year!

# THE GRINCH NEXT DOOR

Most of us try to plan for retirement. Assuming your employer doesn't boot you out the door mere seconds before your pension comes through, you may have put away a few nickels. It's time to do what you would really like to do.

My neighbor, for instance. He loves to garden. When he retired, his yard burst into a flora fest, pristinely maintained with tweezers. As his knees and back have aged, he does less in large patches and more in containers. I believe this is the art form known as growing old gracefully.

I know a political activist who now has the time for the meetings and marches. Sis curls up with all the words she cares to read. I write. All affordable pastimes scaled to life on the Back Nine.

And then there is Neighborhood Grinch one block over. She retired to a life of complaining. Nothing gets past this whiner. When she sees an infraction of the rules, she thunders to her computer to erupt in steam and venom on Next Door and Facebook. Not an infraction of neighborhood rules, mind you ... an infraction of HER rules.

Everyone is a target. Take the housepainter who parks his van in front of his house overnight. Neighborhood Grinch dubbed it an eyesore that will not be tolerated. She's trying to rally neighbors to the cause. My advice to the painter? Move the van before sugar finds its way under the gas cap or a potato up its tailpipe.

We have a street gang of designer dogs on our block. They all look like dust bunnies or the fluff balls of expended dandelions. A new neighbor is desperately trying to teach her mini multi-chon not to yap at the shih-poms and pooch-iranians in surrounding yards. Short of stepping on them all, this will take a while, and she is clearly trying. However, Neighborhood Grinch launched her assault just minutes after the move in.

Now don't get me wrong. We all get miffed. I would prefer people's kitties not stop by to nibble the birds on my feeder. I'm sure something makes you want to fly off the handle. But to Neighborhood Grinch, all life is war. She lectures without end, looking like a female Barney Fife with a very tight perm.

What do you suppose happened in her younger years to make her such a moaner now? What land mind will I trip that will start her on the war path? As soon as I think of it, I will be sure to poke this particular bear.

# THE WRONG CROWD

Before moving to the left side of the country, I spent three decades in Chicago writing ads for clients, national and local. One thing I learned early on is that nobody wants to see your ad, especially if you insist on targeting the wrong audience.

Case in point. This morning I received an email from my insurance company. They've insured me for decades. They KNOW I'm older than Godzilla (the original). And yet they sent me a mailing about motorcycle insurance under the guise of tips for my safe riding.

They started with helpful pointers like this: When you are riding, there's not much between you and the pavement.

Now really. If they kept in mind my age, they wouldn't be saying 'wear non-slip gloves' or 'choose goggles with safety glass.' They'd be saying, "For the love of all that's holy, get the hell off that bike and back up on the porch rocker where you belong."

They wouldn't advise 'know your bike's limits.' They'd say, "Either clear up those cataracts, or you're gonna skin off what's left of your sorry backside when you hit the highway."

I ranted on and on about this until my sister reminded me of a driving trip we took through the Arizona desert. Parched, we pulled into a roadside grocery at the same time a motorcycle gang swept in, on what I believe are called crotch rockets. Colorful. Anyway, as they removed their helmets, we were expecting to ogle a whole bunch of James Deans. Instead, each looked like Gabby Hayes.

So okay, maybe I'm wrong. Maybe my insurance company is right to think I might blossom into Motorcycle Momma or some old man's Old Lady. But in that case, I think I will edit a few of their 'tips' to fit my lifestyle:

Them: Wear shoes that cover your ankles.

Me:Wear shoes that cover your ankles and are cute.

Them: Wear a helmet that meets federal safety standards.

Me:Wear a full body suit the exceeds NASA standards.

Them:Test the lights, brakes and turn signals.

Me:Test the lights, brakes and turn signals. Then get off the bike.

Them: Check the cables to be sure they aren't frayed.

Me:What cables?

Feel free to add to the list. I'm sure you have many fine suggestions of your own before hitting the road on your hog this spring.

# WHY DO IT?

My friend Heidi Hansen and I founded an organization called Olympic Peninsula Authors. We help local writers meet each other as well as readers. In our booth at the Saturday Sequim Farmers & Artisans Market, we feature different independent authors from around the peninsula.

Saturday was cold and rainy and at least three months long if you look at it from the viewpoint of weather. We shared our booth with snails crossing the brick plaza, looking for any place dry. We had rainhats, but none of us thought to bring gloves to MEMORIAL DAY WEEKEND, for heaven's sake.

Authors Heidi, Ruth, Jan, and I huddled together. I'm sure we each wondered what we were doing there. What makes a writer want to share her words so badly that she'll sit in a 10x10 iffy oasis trying to keep books dry?

I know why we do it. We're amazed by the creative talent on the peninsula, be it poets or novelists or children's authors. These are natural born storytellers looking to inform or entertain. I think that, after a career in an office or store, many people finally find their voices at retirement. They've lived enough life to have wisdom to share and the capabilities to do it.

Also, the rise in small presses and/or self-publishing has made it easier to meet readers from your own neck of the woods. And since most creative folks are deeply affected by their environment, it is small wonder so many are drawn to this part of the earth.

I'm more quizzical about what makes visitors come out on a day like Saturday. Fresh produce from local farmers is a great lure, of course. Baked goods, you bet. Tourists have little choice in days; it's now or never. And the market is the Number One spot to walk and socialize dogs. Now what about the rest of you? If you're not a beta tester for raingear, why are you here for non-perishables like purses, dog toys, pottery, keychains, books? What pulls you away from warm beds and hot coffee to trek around in the frigid rain?

It is a kind of bonding, I think. I can't speak for the potter or the woodworker. But as for you readers, you can bet we authors are thrilled to meet you. We envision you at home later in the day in your recliner exploring our pages, your dog now dry at your feet. We've met each other … we are sharing a journey. The appreciation between artists and supporters is such a genuine bond.

We are daily pummeled by news of shootings, war, environmental destruction, rising Covid numbers, gas prices. But on a soggy Saturday in May, at the Sequim Market, visitors and vendors share a day of peace.

# SCAREDY CAT

I agreed to wrangle ten cats on Christmas day. Eight were in one household and two in another. Their owners had out-of-town plans. Even after reading the encyclopedic notes regarding which kitty got which smelly vittles in which bowl, it seemed simple enough. Besides, I had met all these cats. They were fickle felines, none of whom particularly like me. But, you know, any old human holding a food bowl is halfway home. They'd worked up a liking of me before, so I figured we wouldn't hiss at each other.

And that's when the storm hit.

As blizzard wind swelled and snow tumbled, the two cat-owning couples were snowed in. Their schedules changed again and again, breaking and making airline and hotel reservations coast to coast. Meanwhile, I got progressively more worried about those cat bowls on Christmas day. Would I be able to plow out there in my twelve-year-old Toyota? Tensions rose. I didn't say they could no longer count on me; I'd make it somehow.

Eventually, the two couples worked out a deal. One hubby was left to feed kitties as the rest of the humans slogged out to the highway and away. This is a story unto itself, but one for another day. Bottom line, instead of caring for ten cats, I cared for none at all.

I know many of you may believe this was a Christmas miracle, but I actually like cats and would have been happy to do it.

As a result, Christmas day was abnormally quiet. Following decades of noisy ones, I was just fine with the calm. I sat and read and reminisced. Sis and I could even eat what we actually wanted (I far prefer pizza to Brussel sprouts or marshmallows in my yams).

I finally realized something significant had happened after all. This was my first experience with promising more than I could deliver. I would have tried, but it would have scared me to slide in the slush nearly to Joyce and back, if I made it at all. My much younger friends knew that without asking. They looked after ME as well as their cats, although maybe not in that order. Driving in snow like that, well nobody should do it. Especially a senior citizen who doesn't quite realize she is one. There's no doubt age dulls the senses, heightens the glare, slows instinct. I am going to be more careful about what I offer to do now that I am more careful about what I will do. I guess that is a New Year resolution of sorts. A good one.

Besides, cats probably wouldn't start eating each other in just one day on their own. On the other hand …

# CONFESSION OF A PLANT THIEF

I'm not a law breaker. In fact, I'm so far from it that I might not know if I was breaking the law. This explains why I stole plants last spring. At least, I think I did.

Sis is an online bargain hunter. She found camellia bushes at such a remarkable price we bought four of them. All we had to do was pick up and plant. Easy peasy. We drove to the appointed place at the appointed time. It was an apartment building without a garden in sight. Hmmm. After circling the block several times seeking pink blossoms and slick dark leaves, I surrendered. I entered the apartment building parking lot.

The sign on the apartment door should have been a second clue that all was not well in the garden. DO NOT KNOCK. CALL FIRST. Of course, I'd forgotten my cell phone. After a moment of dithering, I did knock but very lightly. Nothing offensive.

Mongo threw open the door, his eyes cutting left then right searching out the SWAT team I'd brought along. I'm tall, but Mongo towered.

"Hello, sir," I squeaked. "I'm here about —"

"Get in here."

He didn't touch me, but I felt dragged through a portal to the dark side. Except, in this case, the dark side was pretty in pink. Camellia bushes filled the living room. Around them were other natural wonders like fig trees and magnolias.

"Wow! Where did you raise all these?" I asked, naïve as a Cabbage Patch doll.

"Get 'em and get out," Mongo growled. I guessed he was not a chatty kind of guy. I hauled the four bushes fast as I could from apartment to car. Mongo did not help, being on guard duty as he was. Sis in the passenger seat showed the good sense to stay there, seatbelt locked at the ready.

On the highway home, I said, "That man sure loves pink flowers."

Sis said, "That man doesn't own them." She used an unpleasant word regarding my brainpower.

I gasped, "You mean?"

"Yes. We've trafficked in stolen landscaping."

"Should I take them back?"

She just stared at me. Of course, you don't return stolen goods to a guy like Mongo. And you sure don't ask for your money back.

This spring, the camellias are blooming in profusion in my yard. They know they're loved. I occasionally picture four empty holes somewhere downstate still awaiting their bushes. I then think shame on me for trusting in low prices. Then I tell myself they weren't stolen, just some sort of camellia overstock sale by Mongo. I have no proof otherwise.

Mostly, when I look at these pops of pink announcing spring is here, I overcome any angst regarding my life of crime, begun in my eighth decade. In fact, if Mongo has any cheap Cherokee dogwoods …

# HAWKING IN THE HEAVENS

Dear Steven:

What are you witnessing now? What answers are igniting your imagination ... what new questions are you spurred to ask? Who does our cosmic thinking for us now that your point of view has so colossally shifted to the other side?

Have you found what is in those black holes? Is one full of missing socks? Another stuffed with all the ethics that don't matter to us anymore?

What about Big Bangs? Are they going off all around you now? Are you inspired by the explosive beginnings of other worlds without end? Parallel universes? Did you have a smooth exit yourself? Do you see a red Tesla passing by? Is it time we all make plans to get out of town?

I did not receive the same long distance vision as you when potential was handed out. I will never comprehend all you tried to teach about gravity and space-time and collapsing stars and other mysteries of the cosmos. I catch glimmers in bursts: I *get* it and then it is gone, the way your eyes lock for a nanosecond on the eyes of a stranger as a passenger train flashes by.

The loss of intelligence is always inconsolable ... through undeveloped potential or age or disease or wanton misuse. The very last thing we need is to lose any more of it. As a species, it feels we are willingly clambering onto the back nine of evolution. For the first time ever, we may have to turn around to see the better view. Can dumbed down humans create AI that is smarter than we are?

Be all that as it may, Stephen, can you now shed some light on the great questions of life? Do you know the way to San Jose? How much is that doggy in the window? Can one-size-fits-all pantyhose actually fit anybody? What is behind door number three? Where is Jimmy Hoffa?

You could not have a Nobel Prize without proof of your beliefs. But do you, at the very least, now have the last laugh?

# Look for other great reads

# by Linda B. Myers

Available through Amazon

eBook or paperback

### *Creation of Madness*

Oregon, 1989. Psychologist Laura Covington takes on a new client who suffers Multiple Personality Disorder (now called Dissociative Identity Disorder). He reveals a vicious cult and the psychopath who rules it. Laura has unleashed dangerous secrets and now must decide how far she is willing to go to protect everything she loves. This psychological suspense will give you chills as it builds toward its unpredictable conclusion...not for the faint of heart.

### *Secrets of the Big Island*

Life is uncomplicated in a Big Island village until Maile Palea, an 8-year-old girl, disappears. Twelve years later she is still missing. This is the story of her sister and brother who never give up trying to find her, of a village that no longer feels safe from a changing world, and a perpetrator who discovers what disasters happen when you keep secrets too long. A perfect read for fans of edgy suspense and hot Hawaiian nights.

## Fun House Chronicles

Self-reliant Lily Gilbert enters a nursing home ready to kick administrative butt until the chill realities of the place nearly flatten her. She calls it the Fun House for the scary sights and sounds that await her there. Soon, however, other quirky residents and caregivers draw Lily and her daughter in as they grapple with their own challenges. Lily discovers each stage of life can be its own adventure with more than a few surprises along the way.

## The Bear Jacobs Mystery Series

The characters in the Bear Jacob Mystery series made their first appearance in *Fun House Chronicles*. PI Bear Jacobs and the rest of the quirky residents at Latin's Ranch Adult Family Home in the Pacific Northwest may be infirm curmudgeons, but all the while, they solve crimes standing tall on their canes, walkers and wheels.

### Mystery One. *Bear in Mind*

Charlie's wife is missing. Is she a heart breaking bitch who abandoned her hubby? Or is a madman attacking older women? When others disappear, Bear and his gang follow a dangerous and twisted trail to a surprising conclusion.

### Mystery Two. *Hard to Bear*

Old-fashioned snuff films reveal a violent new twist: custom-order murder for sale. To stop their creators, Bear's gang joins forces with an avenging mob family, a special forces soldier suffering PTSD, and a pack of mad dogs in the Pacific Northwest woods.

## Novella One. *Bear Claus*

PI Bear Jacobs is mired down with seasonal depression until Lily finds him a mystery to solve. The trail is both fun and fearsome as it leads from theft in the My Fair Pair lingerie shop through a local casino to a dangerous solution in the Northwest Forest.

## Mystery Three. *Bear at Sea*

When Eunice wins the Arctic Angel Award, the Latin's Ranch gang cruises to Alaska to pick up her prize. But high life on shipboard is dashed by low life murderers and thieves. One of their aides is struck down, and Eunice's life is threatened not once but twice.

## Novella Collection: *Three Bears*

Three short mysteries packed in one book. *Bear and the Burrito*: Somebody is dropping off mini-donkeys at Latin's Ranch. Who ... and why? *A Bearable Exit*: Lily's daughter must agree to a most unique proposal to keep rival gangs from threatening Latin's Ranch residents. *Clan of the Craft Bear*: A woodworker is electrocuted while fractal burning. Bear proves it's no accident while grappling with issues that part him from his gang.

## The Slightly Altered History of Cascadia

The spirit Cascadia is created to find the problem with people and fix up what the gods have screwed up. This is a quick-witted romp through history, mythology, and modern day misguidedness. Cascadia is trained in lust by Helen of Troy, in weaponry by Jim Bowie, and much more by other historical types. With help from a flying bear, and a logging horse, Cascadia takes on evil, but can she create a better kind of human ... or will the gods scrap the whole planet?

## Fog Coast Runaway

To escape her dangerous family, young Adelia Wright vanishes on the 1890s Oregon coast. She hides in the scullery of a posh Seaside hotel but is soon on the run again to a logging camp as assistant to the cook, then on to Astoria to sew gowns for the local bordellos in Swilltown. She discovers the love of a collected family can outshine a birth family, and the Tillamook Light guides her way. Historical fiction with strong female leads.

## Dr. Emma's Improbable Happenings

It's 1902 and the hunt for stolen Klondike nuggets leads an outlaw to murder Dr. Emma Prescott's family. She flees Seattle, survives the ill-fated SS Clallam shipwreck, and escapes to the frontier settlement of Port Angeles. She practices medicine, befriends Klallam Willa, suffragettes, and working girls. The outlaw finally catches up with her at Portland's

Lewis and Clark Centennial Exposition. The characters in this novel are fiction, but the history is fact.

## Starting Over Far Away

1921, the Alaska Territory: Nurse Leona arrives at a Tlingit village to help the tribe through frontier plagues. Along with teacher Ivy, the women battle threats from disease, from roughhewn men, from wildlife. Over lemonade and macaroons twenty five years later, Ivy tells the tale to a young amputee fresh from WWII. What became of Leona and what happened to Ivy are revealed along with a past the soldier never knew. A complicated, twisting tale of strong women conquering personal flaws and hazardous circumstances.

# About the Author

Linda B. Myers traded snow boots for rain boots and moved from Chicago to Washington's Olympic Peninsula where she is now part of the old growth. She has published ten novels, is newish to poetry, writes a monthly op/ed piece for the Sequim Gazette, and is a co-founder of Olympic Peninsula Authors, a group devoted to promoting the many fine authors out here in the wild.

Made in the USA
Middletown, DE
29 June 2024

56448732R00066